SAOL AGUS CULTÚR IN ÉIRINN
IRISH LIFE AND CULTURE

CONAMARA

Conamara

SEÁN MAC GIOLLARNÁTH
do scríobh

Pictiúirí ó Láimh
ROWEL FRIERS

Arna chur amach do
Chomhar Cultúra Éireann

ag Cló Mercier,
4 Sráid an Droichid, Corcaigh.

Conamara

by

SEÁN MAC GIOLLARNÁTH

With illustrations by

ROWEL FRIERS

Published for
The Cultural Relations Committee
of Ireland
by the Mercier Press,
4 Bridge Street, Cork.

SBN 85342 297 4
First Edition
1954
Reprinted
1963, 1972

THE aim of this series is to give a broad, informed survey of Irish life and culture, past and present. Each writer is left free to deal with his subject in his own way, and the views expressed are not necessarily those of the Committee. The general editor of the series is Caoimhín Ó Danachair.

Seán Mac Giollarnáth explored all parts of Conamara in search of folktales and local legends and his appreciation of its scenery and wild life grew with acquaintance. Among his publications are *Loinnir Mac Leabhair* (long folktales), *Annála Beaga ó Iorrus Aithneach* (local history), and *Peadar Chois Fhairrge* (memories of an old man). His last book, *Mo Dhúthaigh Fhiain* (My Wild Land) won the Craoibhín Prize and was a Club Leabhar selection. *Saoghal Éanacha* and *Féilire na nÉan* deal with wild birds and their haunts. He made many translations into Irish.

PRINTED IN THE REPUBLIC OF IRELAND BY
LEINSTER LEADER LIMITED, NAAS, CO. KILDARE

CONTENTS

PREFACE

THERE IS A spot in Coisfharaige behind a line of trees that stands between it and the sea. The line was so thin forty years ago that the trees only broke the glistening surface of the bay. Trees are always pleasing to behold, and very often the sea delights the eye, but trees and the sea in proximity are doubly attractive and are exhilarating to the mind. Once on this spot I accompanied An Piarsach walking towards the trees and the sea. As was usual with him he seemed inclined to silence, but suddenly he spoke: "We could have here a little Gaelic kingdom of our own." It had for years been like that with him; in the midst of the most pleasantly distracting surroundings his thoughts were of an Irish-speaking nation. Beside us was a large cluster of houses where only Irish was spoken. Coisfharaige is dotted with such house-clusters, I cannot call them villages. Some of them are alongside the sea road but many are slightly off the road, and in almost every *baile* will be found a seanchaí or storyteller, and often a singer. The same is true of an Ceathru-rua, of Rosmuc and of the peninsula lying beyond Cuan Cille Ciaráin where lies the Carna country. The district which this booklet describes is above all "a little Gaelic kingdom."

GEOGRAPHY AND POPULATION

LOCH COIRIB CUTS the County of Galway in two unequal and dissimilar parts. Conamara, as now generally regarded, includes all that part lying west and north of the lake. Our modern conception of it corresponds very closely to the Iar-Chonnacht described by Ruairi Ó Flaithearta, except that we do not include the Aran

Islands. Aran has distinctions of its own, but the people of Muighinis say, "If you come to Muighinis, see Molrua; if you go to Iorrus Mór, see Cnoc an Airgid; if to Aran, do not omit Eóchaill;" as if Aran were part of their own Conamara. The conformation given the land by the last great disturbance of the earth divides the district sharply into a region of great hills and valleys on the north, and on the south, a region of low-lying, rough moorland with numerous lakes and some isolated and conspicuous hills. The road from Bunnacoille through Crosamháma (Maamcross) to Bailenahinse and Clochán (Clifden) marks the division of these two highly contrasted regions, and the road from Mám eastward to Cornamóna and Cong continues the division and separates the hills of the narrow spur between the lakes of Coirib and Measca from the northern shore of Coirib, Druimsnámh and Dubhros. The valleys in the country of the hills are generally spacious and often impressive because of their precipitous sides, which are bare of all trees, and show a grey face of stone as often as verdant sod. The valley bottoms are occupied by peat bogs or by deep clear lakes, such as Einín, Doire Cláir, and Fuaigh, whose waters are known to all anglers. The lower slopes of the hills have a yellowish, sticky soil that drains ill and gives a rough pasturage not always sweet. Everywhere between the ranges there are extensive moorlands and flat bogs, and beyond the Beanna Beóla the high moor is pierced and restricted and enlivened by long arms of the sea. The hills divide into three groups or ridges. The Beanna Beóla group lies to the west; in the centre is that of Corcóg or Mámtuirc lying between the great valleys of Gleann Einín and Gleanna Mháma; the Líonán ridge runs from the head of the Caoláire to the head of Loch Coirib. This ridge lies in Dúthaigh Sheoigheach and possesses the most rounded hills and provides the most verdant pasture of all three mountain divisions. Outside, on the north, is the great mountain wall of the Formna which is mentioned by Ó Flaithearta as the northern boundary of Iar-Chonnacht.

The hills on their sunny side slope gently down to the edge of the great moorland that extends to Galway Bay on the southern boundary, and from the ocean at Ceann Léime almost to Loch Coirib. The low range of hills from Muigh Cuilinn to Léim beyond Uachtarárd hold it roughly here and shelters the less peaty lands between the heights and the lake. The low moorland is bitten into from the south by sea inlets that reach up to its heart below Crosamháma and Sraith Salach, at Camus and Inver, and again, near Caiseal. Cuan na Beirtrí Buí and that of Clochnarón (Roundstone) almost meet between Caiseal and Tuaim Beóla. These long insinuating inlets carve out many headlands and scatter beauty round an otherwise monotonous land of heather and sedgy lake shores. Marshy boglands encircle lakes great and small, but near the sea, where lakes are less frequent, "the rugged rocks abound", and harsh winds of winter and spring beat down the very lichen that gathers upon them. The rock backbone of the land juts out everywhere, and there are rocks innumerable, dropped by glaciers, singly and in collections as if they had been showered from the sky. Coisfharaige to Casla is studded with these massive boulders, and the noble hill in Seanaféistin, above Clochar lake, is so cluttered with great angular boulders of granite that neither man nor fox can find a straight pathway amongst them. The land between Cnoc Mordáin and the bay of Ciarán is burdened with a similar load of scattered rocks.

Lakes are so numerous that some sheet of fresh water is always in sight. The road from Uachtarárd to Clochán runs alongside a chain of charming trout lakes. Those of

Bailenahinse, Gleanndáloch, Inver, and Scríob are out-rivalled by the famous lochs of Gleannacmuireann and Formaol, all of which have more than a nation-wide fame for white trout and salmon, and for their wild scenery. The long eastern shore of Loch Coirib has endless fishing shallows, and is unsurpassed for free sport.

The climber who ascends Iorrus Beag beyond Cloch-narón, as every visitor should, may see on any reason-ably clear day more lakes than he can easily count. The traveller who hugs the road should halt on the pass of Mám Aoidh, on the way out of the Mám valley, for a view of lakes and moors that may not be had at a lower elevation.

The physical contrast between the two regions described is scarcely more striking than the different ways of life in the valleys of the great hills and by the seashore. The rearing of sheep and cattle is almost the only industry in north Conamara, if we except the eastern spur between Coirib and Measca where the more generous hillsides are industriously tilled. There is no access to the outer sea except in the extreme west where fishing still struggles for existence. There are no dairy herds, no mixed farming, and no cottage industries to speak of. Cattle dot the pastures, and the slopes have flocks of mountain sheep that make the not immoderate wealth of their owners.

The pastoral life gives a similarity of habits and character of the people. The care of mountain flocks is an all-the-year-round concern; it demands many hours in the open, and endless travel on foot. The constant watching in the dropping season, the shearing in summer, the frequent flocking and counting on the fenceless hills, the droving to fairs, make splendid and enduring walkers of boys and men. Walking, indeed, is almost the only physical exercise known amongst the hills, the ground being too uneven to allow riding to be a pleasure. The tempo of the daily round is slow and pleasant. The people are accordingly deliberate and sociable to a high degree, agreeable amongst themselves and welcoming contact with strangers. They have time for a casual conversation that will have few platitudes, and for a story that will be purely imaginative, or for a history that will reek of blood and reality. They know all about the nature and habits of mountain sheep, and all the lore concerning their care. Their independence of character has often been noted, and the northern valleys are famed not only for the best-flavoured mutton, but also for the brainy humans who live therein. Mám valley, it is said, has the cleverest people in Conamara, and the people of Corr, in the valley, are the custodians and expounders of its wit.

The hills draw to their glens the people who live by the rearing of flocks, and these people, if they differ in habits and industry from their neighbours on the small fields around the shore, owe the difference to the single-line industry of hill-grazing rather than to any racial origin attributed to some of them. The people all are Irish, north and south, they speak the same language, and share the same oral literature and traditions.

The seashore has attracted to costal Conamara its numerous population and gives to the people their honourable frugality and tireless industry. The sea in many periods has drawn to its shore fugitives driven by oppression and hunger, for the ocean offered at least food for labour, and labour has remained the lot of the inhabitants of the narrow edges around the Galway coast. The wind-swept islands were occupied and remain occupied. The coast from Bearna to the peninsulas, twenty miles to the west, with their neighbouring islands, is more densely peopled than any other part of Conamara, or indeed of Ireland. It is a paradox to state that the more fertile the soil the fewer the human inhabitants in occupation and employment. The districts of Ceathru-rua, Rosmuc, Cill Ciaráin and Carna have many more families than similar areas in the fertile midlands. St. Patrick, it is said did not visit south Conamara, but viewed it from the height of Mám Éan, and blessed it. He promised that it would have more riches than any other part of the barren land. "Where are the riches?" asked a doubting listener of the seanchaí. "In the people," came the understanding reply. "People were the riches St. Patrick valued."

The poverty of the costal land might suggest that fishing is the staple industry, but this is not so for fishing is only an occasional occupation and the people, men and women, have become versatile in many occupations that provide them with food, fuel and clothing, and that very often enable them to make appreciable savings. The sea, indeed, provides manure for the stony soil. Without the harvest of seaweed there would be no harvest from the land, for it is the weed washed ashore or cut at low tide that enables the industrious worker to grow his potatoes, his patches of corn and meadow hay. The toil of gathering the weed is the most laborious of the year's round. Men plunge into retreating waves to snatch escaping brown hanks, and women, no less zealous carry dripping backloads beyond the high-water mark. No clothes or footwear seem adequate to protect the worker from the soaking salt water, but a sea-wetting never gives a cold. Máirtín Ó Cadhain has given in one of his short stories a grim, unforgettable picture of the toil of the shore.

The gathering of the weed is followed by the sowing of spring. Potatoes, cabbages, turnips, are grown in soil of the poorest. A sparing soil makes a frugal people. The stony ground forbids the use of the plough, and the spade is the instrument of Conamara cultivation. Nowhere else are spade workers so competent and tireless, and the well tempered tool is highly valued. "It would shave a mouse," said a worker of his tempered loy.

The cutting and saving of turf for domestic use and for sale fills another period for the varied toil of the people. Turf production is a summer industry and is never so irksome as the winning of the seaweed. Men do the heavy cutting, and boys and girls find the saving and handling a pleasant adventure in summer air in places fragrant with the warm scents of moorland and sea. The sailing boats that carry turf cargoes are handled by expert boatmen who follow a sailing tradition that has lasted without change for centuries. The large boats are used in carrying weeds from islands where it is piled in great swathes by stormy seas. The running of seaweed to the head of the bay for sale to inland farmers was once an extensive traffic.

Net fishing has not disappeared from Galway bay or the Bófinn sea, but inshore fishing is a profitable if occasional occupation everywhere along the coast. Lobster fishing is profitable, and scallops have brought handsome returns. The long-line fishing from small boats provides a store of fish that is sun-dried and smoked for the long winter.

The men of south Conamara have had useful training and experience in building in the past generation or two. The old dwellings have been largely replaced by new houses of concrete or stone with slate roofing, and it was not found necessary to introduce tradesmen from outside for the work of construction. The characteristic adaptability of workers which has come from the variety of their simple occupations has enabled them, with Government assistance, to establish a successful tomato industry that gives new promise of better times for their barren land. They have turned with success to the learning of new methods of plant cultivation that require more understanding and attention than were necessary for the traditional crops. The numerous glass houses of Cois-

15

fharaige, with their supplies of roof water for inside irrigation, are a most helpful feature of the rock-strewn fields.

A few sheep are kept on every little farm by the shore. They are kept of necessity for their wool, which in south Conamara is the basis of the home knitting and home-spun tweeds. Spinning has not disappeared, nor dyeing and weaving. It is strange that these time-honoured crafts should be more generally practised among the small holders in the south than in the northern valleys where a single farmer may own from one hundred to a thousand sheep, or more. The wool from the hills goes oversea to make American carpets. That of the coastal farms is spun and woven for home wear.

The great social phenomenon of the coastal people—it is phenomenal when we remember the rural inland—is the prevalence of early marriages, large families, and over-flowing schools. The bachelor is far too prevalent in the sheep country, but in the south couples marry in youth, and houses are ever going up. God provides.

SCRAPS OF HISTORY

OUR WESTERN SHORES and valleys were inhabited before the coming of Patrick of the great stride and the fearless demeanour, but we know little of the early dwellers. Unbelievers they were, but one of their chieftains invited the great converter to come to their wild land. The traditional account of his approach which I learned from a reliable man of the Breathnaigh in Mám, differs from that given by Archbishop Healy who states that Patrick came to Mám Éan before going to Cruach Phádraic, and that he came by way of Cong.

St. Patrick entered Conamara, the Mám tradition says, by way of Cill Bríde, Cornamóna and Mám. The moun-

16

tainous approach did not daunt him for he had behind him the challenge of the Cruach, which Thackeray did not meet save in bitter reproach. Tradition says that the Saint was accompanied by St. Martin, but history does not confirm this. Alone or accompanied, however, he held his way, and an unfriendly reception by a tribe at the head of the lake did not deter him from his resolution to reach Mám Éan. No one has traced his footsteps across the Mám river, but he crossed most likely the sandy bed at Braonán. At Mán Éan he made his second retreat on high exposed ground. His bed in a rocky recess is still pointed out. From his lofty view-point he gave his blessing to the moorlands and the distant shores where still lives the memory of his great labours and of his courageous nature.

Another early visitor to this land was St. Colmcille. He came by sea from Aran to Coisfharaige where he found a welcome that must have consoled him for his virtual expulsion by St. Enda. His church was in the townland of Clochmhór. He stands second only to St. Patrick in the veneration of the people. His feast day, June 9th, is the traditional day for the arrival of the salmon shoals of summer. Both Patrick and Colm found rest, or *suaimhneas* on their visits, and *suaimhneas* is the greatest gift Conamara offers to the stranger. Patrick was followed for a century or more by other missionaries, some seeking retreats, and all seeking and making converts. Feichín, the builder of churches in Meath and Sligo, founded his greatest house at Cong, and holy wells and lesser churches preserve his memory in the hills and in the islands of the far west. His name still frequently appears in baptismal registers. Bréanainn, the great adventurer overseas, attracted to Inis Uí Chuinn followers who, like Maoldún, were inspired by his holiness and his adventurous spirit. Bréanainn and Maoldún may have designed and built

17

boats on the islands, and sailed them on the deep waters of the upper lake, the Seanloch. One of the traditional boat builders of Inis a' Ghaill is still alive, and dropped his trade only recently when a nephew took it up in Uachtarárd. Colmán, another traveller, came back from the controversies in Britain to find his share of *suaimhneas* in Inis Bó Finne. The last assaults on the remnants of stubborn unbelievers were made, we may well believe, by Macdara in Iorrus Aithneach, by Flannán in Iorrus Mór, and by Ceannach, who alone suffered martyrdom, in Baile Mhac Conrí and Iomaidh. When Christianity had been generally accepted and communications between the front line missionaries on the Atlantic coast and islands and the responsible seniors in the churches on Loch Coirib kept them in touch with regularising influences. The great road leading from Tara to the west was met by another highway from Sruthar to Sliabh which brought travellers within sight of the great lake. Flannán went to Iorrus Mór from his green island-garden in the lake, Éanna came from Aran to visit Caoillín on Inis Caoillín. Bréanainn was associated with Inis Uí Chuinn, Eanach Dúin and Inis Ní, beyond Tuaim Beola. His church at Eanach Dúin was the cathedral for all Conamara. On the other side of the lake to the east, there were Domhnach Pádraic, Cill Beannáin and Tuaim close by, and within reach by land were all the young centres of the new culture and religion.

The Faith persisted through the dark troubled centuries and the instructions given crystallised into verses still repeated, and parables in sermons became popular tales. The occasional prayers became known to all. Conamara always remained part of Gaelic Ireland. An Ó Cadhla fought with Brian at Cluain Tarbh and the Ó Flaithearta long resisted the Norman barons and their ruthless successors. "Never again" (after a brief alliance with

18

the Normans in 1238), says Gwynn, "was Ó Flaithearta found on the side of the enemy." The harrying of the hill country by the conquerors never ceased for centuries, but the Gael could not be rooted out, and he was reinforced by refugees from East and North after every war. Three unusual refugees, after Cromwellian successes, are mentioned by Ruairí Ó Flaithearta: "Anno 1651, among the many strangers and strange vicissitudes of our own present age, the Marquis of Clanrickard, Lord Deputy of Ireland, the Earl of Castlehaven, and Earl of Clancarty, driven out of the rest of Ireland, were entertained as they landed on the west shore of this lake (Loch Coirib), for a night's lodging, under the mean roof of Murtagh Boy Branagh, an honest farmer's house the same year wherein the most potent Monarch of Great Britain, our present sovereign (Charles II) bowed his imperial triple crown under the boughs of an oak tree, where his life depended on the shade of the tree leaves."

Honest farmer, forsooth: more honest surely than the guests. Charles II rewarded the English yokel who concealed him in the tree with a perpetual pension, paid down to our time, but Ruairí Ó Flaithearta was never restored to the confiscated lands of his father.

Isolated Camus is often referred to as a prison. In the long night of the seventeenth and eighteenth centuries all Conamara was a prison into which dispossessed refugees were driven. It was however a prison with a backdoor that gave exit over the sea to France and Spain. The names of the smuggler-captains are still remembered, and the sites of the signal fires, and the natural habours where the sloops landed their forbidden cargoes are well known.

Bribery and pursuit could not procure the surrender of refugees after the French landing in 1798. O'Connell held a great meeting in Conamara, and the Fenians later got recruits from there. Cóilín Mac Conaola, who ended his long life on Inis Leacan, was a courier carrying arms from Durham to Dublin. He was in Manchester, a lad of seventeen, when Kelly and Deasy were rescued, and like many others had to fly from there the next day. In Durham he and thirty others were arrested for drilling. Anna Parnell was his friend in later years.

Rosmuc associations influenced Pearse largely in his writings, and not a little in his national ideals. In the later fight for Freedom the Conamara column did not falter in its isolation. Two of its members have left us records in Irish of its effort and trials. That of Colm Ó Gaora is well known. The short account of the late Professor Tomás Ó Máille is a classic of personal experience.

ROADS TO TRAVEL

"THE CLIFDEN CAR, which carries the Dublin letters into the heart of Conamara, conducts the passenger over one of the most wild and beautiful districts that it is ever the fortune of a traveller to examine . . . The best guidebook that was ever written cannot set the view before the mind's eye of the reader . . . All one can do is to lay down the pen and ruminate and cry, 'Beautiful'; once more." So wrote Thackeray in *The Irish Sketch Book*.

The railway when it came, long after the appearance of *The Irish Sketch Book*, ran alongside the Galway-Clifden road because, it was reasoned, the road engineer had found the most suitable levels. It avoided the populous districts, it brought no prosperity, no dividends, and it has disappeared. The more modern bus and motor car have taken its place, and all roads admit of transport to suit all travellers. The walking traveller belongs to a past age, for even the hiker will take any conveyance rather than foot it. Pádraic Ó Conaire, trailing after his *asal beag dubh*, and the American artist who walked the roads of Conamara, may go into tradition as the two last foot-travellers of Ireland, as Caoilte and An Bodach figure in earlier memories.

The visitor who would see the wildest glens and the great panoramas—and the glens are of the wildest and the panoramas are great and varied in Conamara—must be prepared to walk and climb. The paths through the glens are not unpleasant and the most commanding hill tops are accessible without cliff climbing. Few glens are without a family or two and very few of them are without cliffs of desolation that present the harsh side of Mother Earth, and make one wonder why in her most inhospitable places she will make a pool deep and sheltered for trout, or induce a companionable man to make a home. The search for trout or for a good storyteller has led the writer into many out of the way places and the reward has always repaid the tramp and the climb.

The roads lead everywhere: to Coisfharaige, and Casla; to the land of lakes and fish above Casla; to Rosmuc of Pádraic Ó Conaire, and Piarsach and Colm Ó Gaora; to Carna and ever-famous Iorrus Aithneach; to Clochnarón and Iorrus Beag; to the wild coast south and north of Clochán; to the surprising Mám valley; and to the way above the Caoláire beyond Líonán; to the circular way round the Beanna by Coill Mhór; and to the high land between Clonbur and Cornamóna from which one may view the wooded islands of Loch Coirib set in their noble lake.

The lasting impression left by a visitor to any wild region may be influenced by the first impression received, and the first view obtained by the traveller who selects the level road from Galway is gradually formed passing by pleasant lakes and low hills, with the caps of the higher mountains beckoning from the distance. The more distant

21

Mayo mountains also show their outline and it is always a joy on this Galway-Uachtarárd highway to catch on a clear day the shape and curve of Néifinn Mhór. It may be seen also at the height of the road from Carraig to Clonbur. I know of no other isolated hill so fine if it be not Sliabh Coimeálta beside the lower Shannon. Néifinn is not a Conamara possession, but the views of the mountains beyond her borders are as much her scenic wealth as are the Beanna Beóla at her centre, and the external views include Cruachán in Acaill, the island of Cliara and Cnoc Bréanainn in Ciarraighe.

The view of Loch Coirib from the road to Uachtarárd is seldom a good one. The road to the left at Muigh Cuilinn leads directly to higher ground which gives a full view of the lower lake, and the great Achré beyond, with Cnoc Meá guarding the plain and housing the *Sidhe*.

At Uachtarárd a road to the right leads by the shore to Corrach Riabhach and Gleann. This lakeside road, not ten miles in length, is a cul-de-sac which lies through the most beautiful scenes of lake, islands and mountains. The view from Corrach Riabhach to Cong embraces many tree-clad islands, including Inis a' Ghaill, known for its Christian antiquities. At the end of the drive the lake has narrowed to a neck, and on the opposite side the wooded hill of Dún sits below the higher hills of the north shore. The long flat-topped mountain of Beann Shléive is imminent beyond the lake all along this detour.

You may only join the main road again at Uachtarárd where you will cross by an ancient bridge the wide shallow river that is the spawning bed of salmon and trout, the great attraction of this little town. As you drive beneath the trees of the riverside you leave behind you the little, green, walled fields and will not behold a tree or rich pasture again for many miles. The peaks of northern hills will come into view, and lakes on right and left will break the monotony of heather and fern.

At Crosamháma you may halt to consider which of the roads to follow. The road to the right over the pass of Mám Aoidh between Leac Aimhré and Corcóg. leads into the grandest of Conamara glens and to Líonán beyond. You will advisedly leave exploration of the region over for a special day. The road to the left leads to Rosmuc and by Cill Ciaráin to Carna, and these centres may be covered on a return journey by the sea road. On the main road you will pass close to Loch Sindile beneath the Corcóg. It has a large wooded island and is valued for white trout fishing no less than for its picturesque setting. On the left the hill of Úirid stands over the lake of Úirid and is the height around which local prophecy says the last battle for Christianity will be fought, when at last the forces of evil will be destroyed. The tale of Tomás Buí of Úirid tells how a man of the Joyces outwitted an Ó Máille. The Joyces were reputed to have small slender hands, and Ó Máille in completing a marriage agreement for his daughter consented to give the suitor a handful of sovereigns from the *sciléid*. Joyce proposed that he himself should dip into the treasury, to which Ó Máille, thinking of the small hands of the Joyces, agreed. This particular Joyce had a hand so large that it grasped most of the money in the pot, but this was the only known instance in which one of his race ever outwitted a man of the older clan.

The hill of Caiseal on the south of the road ten miles ahead is isolated from the mountains and for that reason is more conspicuous than any of the Beanna. It is a shapely hill, well under one thousand feet. In frosty weather when wind and water are calm, one of the roadside lakes will show this height inverted in the water, with all its colours reproduced and, at close quarters, showing any movement of man or beast about the summit.

The reflection of hills in lake water is not peculiar to Conamara, but hill and lake are so plentiful here that the sight may often be enjoyed in winter when during frost the still water and clear sky make a perfect mirror.

You will notice a clump of trees at Sraith Salach where the river, the old railway track and the public road approach each other between Lios Uachtair and the lake of Gleanndáloch. Over the trees, before you drop to the lower level of the road, you will catch sight of Beann Bhán. Its perfect cone distinguishes it from all other neighbouring peaks. It is the highest and proudest of them, and modestly stands back from the front line as if confident of its own superiority. When you are in Gleann Einín you will find an easy path to its top. Gleanndáloch has a homely hotel in the trees beyond the lake and facing the mountains. The wooded hill behind the hotel is an unguarded bird sanctuary, and there is a brown trout lake in a hollow, where fishing is free. The fox and *broc* haunt the thick shrubbery; and in early morning hares may be seen on the back pastures. You have decided to leave Gleann Einín and Coill Mhór for another day, and proceeding you will pass on your right the road leading between the Mám range and the Beanna, and soon after, within two miles or less, you will pass on your left the road to Carna and Caiseal, and that to Clochnarón at Liosnabrucaí. The beauty of this spot of river, lake and wood, at the foot of the most southern of the Beanna, is so surprising that the traveller is constrained to delay. There is a large modern house in the trees above the lake. A lady who lived there painted a set of Stations of the Cross for the little chapel at the end of the late. The main road is carried over the river by a high bridge under which white trout and salmon pass in season up to the lakes of Doire Cláir, Einín, Gleanndáloch and Úirid. The banks below the bridge make a level foot-hold for the fortunate angler who is allowed the freedom of this stream when fish are moving to the larger waters.

The road continues past the long lake of Bailenahinse, and by the young and thriving plantation that belies the belief that Conamara has no visible soil for trees. The modern hotel stands within the woods on the Abhainn Mhór, a salmon river of great worth in every sense. It is a fast stream, with famous pools in its few short miles to the sea at Tuaim Beóla. Bailenahinse was first an Ó Cadhla possession. The Ó Flaithearta enjoyed it for long until Bingham, an English governor, slaughtered there all the leading men of the clann. The Ó Flaithearta had built and endowed a monastery, a centre of religion and education. The Martins, who followed in possession, pulled it down, it is said, and built a prison of the material. The family have been publicised by various writers for an English public. In the most Gaelic part of Ireland they remained un-Irish. They collected large rents in shillings, but created no lasting benefits for themselves, or for their numerous tenants. They never were priest-hunters or hangmen, as were the hated Binghams and Browns, and local tradition tells that they were not unwilling to intercede for clemency for outlawed men to whom Conamara often gave refuge. They were extravagant and spendthrift. The most famous of them was known as Humanity Martin because of his campaign for kindness to animals. Misfortune tracked him as a debtor. W. B. Yeats celebrated in "Colonel Martin" the disgrace brought upon him by his deserting wife. It is strange that this sadly comic story is almost the only one of the Colonel that is still vividly told by Gaeilgeóirí of the district. The last of the Martins died while relieving famine victims, and his gifted daughter died in poverty, an exile in New York.

At the centre of the wood a narrow lane leads to the

hotel. It is well worth while following this lane, and if you go past the hotel door until you reach the bridge over the river you may enjoy a rare view. If the stream be not in spate, go down into its stony bed and look upriver between the trees. You will behold an imminent mountain looking very steep and shapely, set in a sylvan frame. The picture is not surpassed by anything else at Baile-nahinse outside its luxurious hotel.

You must go to An Clochán if only to look back from there upon the Beanna Beóla. They are sufficiently far away from the little town to make their clustering peaks impressive. They are not so pointed as the many peaks of Western Scotland, nor so massive as the Cevennes, but they form a noble hill-group of granite and gneiss.

SCENERY

WRITERS ON TRAVEL try to convey the impression which the impact of a strange land makes on their minds. Intimate and long acquaintance with scenes described give substance and colour to the author's account or word picture, but a flying visitor can gather only fugitive features of hill and valley. The reader is not often given the resident's valuation of the scenery of his native fields. Generally, such valuation fails to reach publication or even deliberate expression, and yet it is the authentic appreciation which explains in some degree the attachment of a people to grudging soil and unsheltered shores. Once in a district where every inhabitant was known to me I saw a girl, then on the very eve of her departure for

27

America, walking pensively alone by the shore of a lake which had been familiar to her, with all its wooded islands, since first she could walk abroad. I had expected her to have been busy in preparation for her long journey, or saying a last farewell to relatives and friends. As I approached she said, as if in anticipation of my surprise, "I am taking with me the full of my eyes,"—*tá mé a' tabhairt lán mo shúl liom*. She had become conscious of the scenes that were dear to her, although she may never before have spoken of them, and she knew that in exile the vivid memory of them should be an unfailing comfort. Most exiles depart without such deliberation, but they undoubtedly try in pensive moments to recall the scenes of youth. An exile who had returned from America early in life told me that all his dreams while away had been of the little fields of home. He would see them, as if from air, the quilted hillsides, and the shore stripes with their walled boundaries, and the green patches around the grey rocks. He also had taken with him "the full of his eye." The exile from Conamara never thinks that his land is anything but beautiful. It still remains as it came from the hands of the Creator.

Rainbow colours may be seen more often than the rainbow but not in its violent contrasts. The yellow of the furze, the red of the fuchsia, the scarlet of the rowan, the purple of the heather, the pinks of rhododendrons and the creams of many blooms will make a generous display, but not all together in time or place. The roadsides and slopes are brightened by the green and gold of the furze from February to high summer. The fuchsia of the red and purple flower is almost a vanity in its display. Its drooping, tender bloom and pale stems are not peculiar to our mild climate, although they prosper in it, and the shrub has never spread over whole acres as the whins have done. The demonstrative rhododendron has gained

a firm hold amid the greys, greens and purples of Coill
Mhor, it has colonised Corr Uí Mhongáin, and is
luxuriant in spots about Mám and on the road east to
Cong.

We have no flowering chestnuts or great beeches, but
the humble rowan is treasured for its creamy bloom in
summer and its wealth of shining red fruit in early
autumn, brighter than haws and less glaring than cherries.
The holly is even more solitary than the rowan, for single
trees find root in the most desolate places, birds scattering
the fruit stones in their wanderings. The planting, of
course, repays the planter, for the holly berry is a good
winter standby for blackbird, thrush and redwing. A
single, starved holly bush on a stony hillside or on a lake
islet is here as important as the beech on the lawn. The
vivid green tree or clump in a waste of sedge has an
exaggerated colour-value in summer, when it is an
emerald, and in winter, when it becomes a cardinal of
the evergreens. Its foliage makes it conspicuous at all
times in grey surroundings. The berries come to their
richest radiance in December when in defiance of all
weather the tree sprouts its lovely decoration. There is a
shapely holly tree of great size on a hillside above Mám
that on dark winter days glows like a slow fire with the
mantle of clustered fruit that hides its prickly leaves.
Both rowan and holly make, here and there, a border
for the woods of Bailenahinse.

The thickets of hazel, birch and hawthorn by Loch
Coirib have little beauty, but they give cover to woodcock,
and security to badger and fox. In former days they made
a safe retreat for small-scale portable distilleries. Many of
the fishing lakes have inlets covered to the water's edge
with stunted trees in which herons, hawks and the grey
crow nest, and with flowering shrubs, reeds and tall
unbrowsed grasses. A stunted hydrangea produces its

flower-cluster among the rocks. Dwarf willows remain for ever diminutive, and pockets of peat or clefts in the granite support a varied population of flowering plants and herbs. The ling and heather give the prevailing colour to the moors, high and low, but it is the bonny common heather that fills autumn with its restrained brightness, so beloved of our artists. St. Davock's and Mackay heathers have made Iorrus Beag famous among the botanists. The spearlike loosestrife creates a crimson blaze on almost every bank, guarded by the tall royal fern in uniform of the greenest dye, or by irises in yellow caps. Londonpride festoons rock facings, and has spread over the moist and shady spots of Coill Mhór and Muighárd. On low ground unattractive sedges bear ears of shining seed almost as large as flax seed, which the wild-duck greedily gobbles. The common fern in summer green or autumn red has little to attract the eye, but it hides the hare and the stoat, and beds in winter the domestic beast where straw is never in supply. Specks of coloured bloom on plants known only to the botanist make mozaic beds on many bleak surfaces.

The white strands of southern and western Conamara make a modest effort to present some floral decoration. The sea holly and marsh mallow are easily found, seapinks love the shore and an observant eye will pick out eye-bright, dwarf pansies and violets above high water-mark. Saxifrages love poverty of soil and this they find easily and flourish on it.

MORE ROADS TO TRAVEL

WEST CONAMARA HAS the advantage that it may be explored from any of the well known centres, Carna, Caiseal, Gleanndáloch, Bailenahinse, Clochán, or Líonán, but Clochán is the pivot for most journeyings. Every bay and inlet call the traveller, but he will be wise to do his trip northward before beginning his tour of the coast road that leads back to Galway. The road to Muighárd. Leitirfraig and Salroc passes between the mountains and the sea, by many winding inlets with shores less barren than the heathery hills, and affording views from high ground that delight a traveller from a tamer land. Time is necessary for undesirable detours. The journey round by An Tulach is unavoidable, for you want to see from Salroc the mountain Maolré. It is the highest hill in Connacht and rises from the sea just across the mouth of the Caoláire. On the road by Loch Fé you will see a lake island where once Sir William Wilde had a summer lodge. At Coill Mhór the steep height above the castle and the lake will startle you more than the massive building. The run down Gleann Einín will show you the long regular line of the great Beann Bhreacáin, and many other heights to right and left. Your road is always level, and from halfway down the long gleann it runs for miles beside the lake of Loch Einín which holds so many trout and salmon that its fame amongst anglers makes it yearly more valuable. Lios Uachtair, at the end of the valley which it guards, holds the beds of green marble which we admire but seldom use.

Gleann a' Mháma, the Mám valley, should be entered from Crosamháma by the road over the pass between Leic Aimhré and Corcóg. At the height of the road the view of the green-brown gleann suddenly opens between the hills that send down their stream to its winding river. On the right are green Log an Ime, because of its pastures, and at the other end, Roighne or Great Face· The road downwards from the pass heads straight for the towering hill above the bridge at which you turn left up the valley. The small house of the late Micheál Breathnach stands on the side of the road not far from the bridge and looking across the valley. The owner was a gifted storyteller and a most entertaining companion. The Corcóg or Mám Tuirc range beyond the river holds the view all the way from Corcóg to Log Mhám Té, and Cnoc na Lí and Breacán. On the floor of the gleann stands Cnoc na Coire, with its angry face, called Aill na gCat, because there the wildcat had its last haunt. Behind this hill in the valley lies Gleann Fhada, known to few save the walking shepherd, and beyond the sloping back of Corr lies Gleann Glaise, an almost trackless but inhabited region where the wild deer held a retreat for long, and where the last wolf was slain. It was above this hidden gleann that Feichín, the church builder, blessed the well that still sparkles. The road approaches the river at Braonán where the bridge carries the narrow lane that leads into Corr. It was here over the sandy ford that St. Patrick may have crossed the stream on his way to Mám Éan, west of the Corcóg. In late summer and September the brown trout from Loch Coirib make their way to the most distant pools of the rivers. In Muintir Eóin was fought one of the first engagements in the Fight for Freedom beside the birthplace of the noted scholar, Tomás Ó Máille. Sruthán na Lí, above Muintir Eóin, is a famous trout stream to which there is a rush of anglers after early autumn floods. The hills on every side, less barren than the Beanna, are dotted with sheep, the hardy horned variety that give the sweetest mutton.

In this land, tradition tells, there once lived a wealthy sheep farmer who gathered about him twelve wives and, with great foresight, provided for each a separate dwelling Which his clann was I do not not know, but he lives in folklore by the name of Pádraic na mBan.

The road by Líonán leads up by the noble, sheltered Caoláire which is banked on the Mayo side by the lofty Síofra and the ridge that stands over the dark Delphi valley over which Maolré rises on the west.

The road to Loch na Fuaighe begins halfway through Gleanna Mháma. It is the most hilly road in Conamara, but is safe for cycle or car, and it leads into the wildest scenery past Tom na Há, and by Seanafarachán, with its houses on the shore of the lake, where descendants of Norman and Gael, now as Gaelic as each other, live in happy peace with great frugality, and who offer to visitors the kindly hospitality so highly praised by Stephen Gwynn.

If you would keep within Conamara you must take the road by Finne and Clonbur. While the visitor is in the Clonbur district, or staying at Cong, he should explore the four thickly populated townlands called the Four Duachtaí. They lie within the hills, guarded by Beann Shléive, and the hill of Cromghlinn. The way to the Duachtaí lies through Cornamóna. From there an easy ascent can be made to the flat top of Beann Shléive which commands the view of Measc as well as that of Coirib, and of the rugged Dúthaigh Sheoigheach, or Joyce Country. From Clonbur the road to Carraig and Mám will take you over the high land over-looking the broadest and finest part of Loch Coirib. The scene, with the wooded islands, and beyond, the land of Gleann Iar-Chonnacht and Currach Riabhach, is not excelled in this land of scenery. Breandán the voyager, Maoldún, of literary fame, and Fursa the missionary to Peronne, were associated with these islands. A nephew of Patrick's lies beneath a pillar stone in Inis a' Ghaill.

On the wooded hill of Dún is the grave of a legendary queen, and below Mám Cloch a' Luain, Caisleán na Circe stands on a small island close to the shore.

STORM AND CLOUD

CONAMARA GETS ITS share of fine weather, when the wild bloom and scenery of valley and hill may best be enjoyed, but there are many sorts of weather here by the Atlantic, and the experience of a great storm is something to remember. The open sea is often driven to the wildest extravagances which only the staunch cliffs and rocks restrain. Ceann Léime, in the extreme west, sends out a chain of rocks into the open sea and here, when the storm breaks over them, the greatest upheavals of wave and spray may be seen from the lighthouse or from the solid mainland. The headland had an evil reputation for wrecks in sailing days, in spite of the protection of St.

Caoillín whose little church and well are nearby. His feast day is on November 13th, which is about the beginning of ocean inclemency. "Born for Ceann Léime," was said to be the fate most feared by the English mother for her sailor sons. Nor have native boatmen been always safe. Less than a generation back a whole fleet of boats was swallowed in a sudden storm off this coast. Wreckage came into every little bay during the recent great wars and tradition tells of many disasters within the more sheltered waters of Galway bay. Dúirling na Spáinneach witnessed the breaking of a Spanish ship, of the Armada it is supposed, with two hundred men who were saved only to meet their official execution by the English garrison of Galway. A great anchor may still be seen at the base of the Sceird Mhór, opposite Dúirling na Spáinneach. Cuan an Fhir Mhóir, farther up the bay, brought death to one hundred souls and their pilot, Tuathal Ó Máille, in 1560. Many *caoine* songs, such as that for Liam Ó Raghaille, tell of smaller disasters, and there is a reliable account of a volunteer crew which sailed an emigrant ship to America after her captain and men had deserted her in mid-ocean. The crew of volunteers came from Leitir Mealláin, their captain was a Mary Fitzpatrick, and the mate was a daughter of a celebrated smuggler named Ó Máille.

Ara Bheag (Hy Brazil) may not be visible in inclement weather, but inland, the floating fog blankets will give the illusion of islands in the sea in places where you know there are solid hills. The vapoury veil will sometimes halo a peak like Beann Bhreacáin without hiding its crown, or it will cloak half a mountain side until scattered by the wind. When the peaks are snow-clad you may behold a succession of colours from the lower ground upwards. Beside you, the faded green of the sedges prevails. On the lower slopes the brown heather has become a dark purple, and the greenery of the ferns has changed to red.

Between the last vegetation and the summits the rock of the mountains stands in its unchanging dull grey, and above two thousand feet the pure white of the winter cap contrasts with all the colours below.

When heavy clouds touch down to the mountain tops the fisherman on Loch Dhoire Cláir or Loch Einín knows that he may as well retire to the nearby inn, or go home, for the overcast sky stops fishing, although white trout will take readily in pelting downpour, but seldom on a heavy day. The foggy mist makes the most unwelcome of weathers, yet, when the morning sun pierces through, it will open vistas of vivid hues that may not often be seen. Painters have made us familiar with Conamara blues and purples, but there are bright greens that are seldom caught because they are as fugitive as the sun ray through the morning mist. Once at Glenndáloch as we looked across the lake towards the hill of Lios Uachtair a window opened in the enveloping mist that hid base and summit, and, framed in that window, far up the hillside we saw a white-walled cottage and little meadows of the brightest green and a few patches of yellow corn. It was like an illustion, for the window in the mist closed almost instantly and all was grey again; but the memory of the picture remains.

Winds in the mountains can be discomfort to birds and animals no less than to men. Dead seabirds have been found far inland battered on cliff faces after great gales. Wild geese are often forced to reverse on their course without being able safely to turn. The little songsters, the twite and the redpole, and the chats cling to the heather or hide among the stones when winds race and whirl. A blast in the narrow valleys or exposed slopes will lift a sheep so high into the air that the return fall will be fatal; but the low houses hold to their foundations in every storm. In deep valleys the air current gathers a vast momentum and hail comes down like frozen rods. The writer on an unusually bad day was forced into shelter near the bridge at Mám. He saw advancing up the gleann a curtain of white hail, extending from range to range and driven by a roaring wind. As the storm passed over, the few poplar trees by the roadside bent over as if they were willow rods.

THE ROAD BY THE SEA

THE WEATHER IN Conamara is sometimes very dry, but enjoyment may be found in interesting places in most weathers. If the weather be too dry and you wish to see the water-fall in Abhainn Glinne at Clochán you will pray for a deluge, for there is no better display to be seen on any of our rivers than is shown here when the river is in flood. The short river from Gleanndáloch to Doire Cláir passes over a fall and through a deep gorge where it makes a noisy but confined row between the high rocks on either bank. The Abhainn Mhór below Bailenahinse swells its bosom broadly but silently, even in flood. The fall at Seanamhóinín above Spidéal is a great howler in the wood, but, again, it is confined by high banks of rock. The fall at Clochán has a broad, projecting, rugged breast, much higher than the banks below, and it is the thunderer of all our falls.

White trout may be seen at the head of the salt lake of Árdbéara where they wait for a spate in the stream that comes from the lakes of Dúinín. The road to Dúinín leads up the hill to the old village site. Formerly it went round the inlet, before the narrow neck below was bridged. Only one house now remains, but the walk through the topsy-turvy hills is worth while for the view over and beyond Loch Árdbéara. It was here after the war of 1798 that the outlaw, Father Maoilre Prendergast, found refuge. The cottage, still inhabited, is that in which he lodged. A spy who had known him tracked him to this last retreat. It was the tracker who perished.

The road round the coast through Baile Maconaola passes close to Iorrus Fhlannáin, and by a large strand of yellowish vegetable coral. Time should be borrowed to go through Iorrus Fhlannáin, if only to discover how wild and rugged a land of crags may be. It once attracted a saint who gave it his name; but when a poet, the celebrated Mac Suibhne, sought a night's lodging there, it would have none of him. He paid, nevertheless, for the bed refused him in a scalding satire. The refusal of shelter was a mistake, for the author of *An Púca* and *Banais Pheigi Ní Eaghra* could have been very entertaining by the fireside.

The road from Baile Maconaola to Clochnarón skirts a rugged coast looking out on the Atlantic. It passes over a small river that allows salmon and trout to run up during floods to the small lakes on the left of the highway. Domhnall Ó Fotharta while teaching in the local school here gathered the tales and songs contained in *Siamsa an Gheimhridh*. He was a most unusual sort of teacher for his time and place, for he picked up literary gold where others of his day found nothing, and left nothing.

The modern dwellings have slated roofs and are similar in type almost everywhere in Conamara. A few specimens of the old type of house may still be seen along this wild coast. Evans, in *Irish Heritage*, quotes the tribute to the old style of dwelling by a Swedish author:

"Lacking nearly every architectural consciousness and at the same time every kind of imported building material, the Irish peasant house never stands out in bold relief against its background but melts into it even as a tree or rock. Wherever the old building traditions are faithfully maintained its features are a

39

fine simplicity. The best thatching gives the finest peasant roof in Europe."

At the little wood of Murbhe the road turns sharply to the shore and the pleasant little bays and white strands about the green headland of Goirtín come suddenly into view.

Beyond them are the tall island of Cruach na Caoile and the lower but more venerated one of Macdara, where his church still stands and where this locally popular saint lies buried in his "inviolable sanctuary", as Ó Flaithearta calls it. The building is very ancient and the roof of stone might easily be restored, for part of it still remains. It is one of the rarest specimens of our early church architecture and should be seen by everyone who visits this coast. The hill of Iorrus Beag overlooks the bays and islands, and a land of little brown-trout lakes that lies behind it. Praeger and other writers have made it famous for the rare heathers that grow on its slopes. Clochnarón village sits at the opening of the inlet that runs up to Tuaim Beóla where it receives the waters of Abhainn Mhór and to which it brings the salmon and trout shoals as regularly as the summer comes.

Inis Ní, long and humpy, lies opposite across the narrow bay. From here came the wife of Tadhg na Buile of Áird, she who so little regretted his murder. The exactions of Tadhg na Buile drove the son of a widow to desperation, but the oppressor kept safely within the walls about his castle, which was at the head of Cuainín na hÁirde. There was no fresh water supply within the walls and the door leading to the well outside was left open at night by a servant. Through the open doorway the murderer came armed with a dagger and found his way to Tadhg's bedroom where he stabbed him in his sleep. It was said that his wife regretted the bloody linen more than the loss of her husband. Inis Ní was once forest land. Four different

40

varieties of timber have been dug out of its poor soil. A house of the Dominican Order was founded here when Ó Flaithearta held Bailenahinse, and St. Breandán had followers in this neighbourhood, for his name is still connected with the island.

The road out of Clochnarón to Bailenahinse and Caiseal looks towards the Beanna Beóla and commands many of the finest views in Conamara. Before parting with the village street one may on inquiry discover the house above the road where Seán Mac Conrí, the story-teller, died a few years ago. Seán had lost his sight in early life through an accident in an English coal mine. He was cared for in his old age by a sister and was always perfectly dressed in bréidín and white linen. He never wore boots in the house, but the heaviest of home-knit socks, and he always sat on the same side of the kitchen fire. His face expressed more than resignation, it was a happy face. When alone, he would tell his beads silently. When a neighbour came in he made lively conversation, and he could recognise every neighbour by his voice. Strangers who came more than once he learned to recognise as soon as they greeted him. He had a store of literary tales, and it was he told the writer a fine version of *Diarmuid and Gráinne*. He knew a number of traditional prayers and had a knowledge of history. His national feeling led him to join the Fenian Brotherhood while in England. Seán Mac Conrí was a *duine uasal* who needed no prayers on his departure.

From the door of the cottage where he lived one may see some of the hundred views that met the critical eye of Thackeray on his journey from Bailenahinse to the local courthouse. The Beanna in outline remind us of Merriman's line:

'*Ag bagairt a gcinn thar druim a chéile,*'

41

or that of Yeats:
"Come where hill lies heaped upon hill,"

but poet or painter must fail to picture their ever-changing colours. A child seeing them for the first time in twilight exclaimed, "Does God walk along the great peaks at night?"

We see, looking east from here, the isolated hills of Caiseal and Úirid, and the two hills of Carna, Coillín and Cnoc Buí, and across the cuan of Beirtreach Buí are Béacán and Mordán.

The road turns to the right at Tuaim Beóla bridge for Caiseal. The coast on the way is full of interest and has pleasant homes facing the sun and sheltered by the hills. The hotel stands near the turn for Carna.

Iorrus Aithneach peninsula has so many cultural attractions in its singers and storytellers that an unbroken stay of twelve months would not exhaust them. How the great body of folklore that has been forgotten in many countrysides came to be known and preserved in the little homes from Leitirárd across to Cill Ciaráin is a problem for specialists who have time to investigate the meandering ways by which tales travel. The eager student of Irish could find no better university than a fireside here in Coillín, or Ruisínnamainiach, Aillnabrón, or Loch-conaora, with some successor of Éamon de Búrca, Micheál Mac Donnacha, Seán Ó Briain and the other master storytellers whose tales have been recorded for the Folklore Commission. A living singer has given one collector as many as fifty songs, including words and music. The visitor who comes to this district with some knowledge of the Irish language will be able to share in the common culture of the people. The privilege of intimate communication with the inhabitants of any land having a distinctive culture affords more lasting pleasure than any other attractions that it can offer.

Iorrus Aithneach has many lakes, sea inlets, strands and islands about the coast, and if its own hills are only of moderate height, the Beanna are always in view. The hills above Aillnabrón command finer views of broken coast and islands and of lakes and moors than any other heights, and passable roads cross from the Carna side to that of Cill Ciaráin. Carna hotel is the centre from which roads radiate to Muighinis, Muighros and Áird, Glinsc, Aillnabrón and Cill Ciaráin, and to the series of trout lakes west of Cnoc Mordáin.

The road to Coisfharaige and Galway leads along Cuan Cille Ciaráin to Pearse's adopted land of Rosmuc. The cottage he had built at Gortmór indicates the simplicity of the life he desired. It stands beside a small lake in which brown trout abound. The famous fishing lakes at Inver and Scríob never attracted him. The high hills may be seen from the cottage door, and between the cottage and the sea the land is as uneven and desolate as any inhabited region in Ireland. It was here that the latest prophet of our nationality used to come for rest and inspiration. It was here that he learned to find the way to the heart of his countrymen.

The road to Galway by Coisfharaige passes through the most thickly settled part of Conamara, and the bay is always in sight, and the hills of Clare. The traveller has not been told all about local history or geography, but he should have visited Cong because it contains the greatest remains of western architecture; and Eanach Dúin where Bréanainn died, because it was the cathedral city of Conamara; Macdara island, because it contains the very famous church of the saint; and An Spidéal which has in its new church an example of our new architecture in the design of Scott from Eanach Dúin.

43

GATHERINGS

GATHERINGS OF THE people may be seen on Sundays, on fair days, on festival days at holy wells and occasionally at boat and pony races. Games or sports are little practised in Conamara for the rugged ground forbids them. The only level dry ground is the roadway, unless we regard the strands which are so level in a few places that horses are safely raced on them. The pony races on the strands at Iomaidh, Leitir Geis and Baile Maconaola attract many spectators. The happiest gatherings of all are those of the school children. Thackeray who had so many cynical things to say about us confessed that in Conamara he found the love of children very remarkable. He wrote of the tenderness shown them and of the toleration for their childish pranks. The happy faces and disposition of Conamara children are no doubt largely due to the kindness of their parents, but teachers and school regulations no longer repel the not inconsiderable knowledge which children take with them to school. The song learned by the fireside at home, and the traditional tale, are encouraged in the school, so that the young suffer from no feeling of inferiority in the presence of the teacher. The improving teacher is even seeking their assistance in building up his knowledge of music, of local history, of botany and of the Irish language itself. The fruits of such an understanding attitude towards our traditional culture must be manifold. It is only in the Gaeltacht that the homes can give substantial contributions to the work of the school for in the greater part of Ireland where the Irish language is no longer known, the songs and music, the old tales, and all the traditional lore of rual life have almost disappeared. I remember long ago visiting a school in company with the late Edward Martyn. It was before the happy change in our primary education had

come about. His name and love of music were known to the teachers, and the girls' choir was lined up to sing in Irish. The performance did not win his praise. The teacher in charge then called from a back bench two girls who could sing in the traditional way but who had been excluded from the trained choir. They sang to an old air of considerable difficulty which greatly charmed the distinguished visitor. We discovered that the girls were sisters belonging to a family famous for generations of singers.

The Sunday Mass is a great occasion for the coming together of all, of children and of grown people of both sexes. The roads from the chapel will be crowded with two separate sections, the women and girls who hurry away, the men and boys who disperse more slowly. Conversation after the silent hour in church will have no restraint. There will be no display of shabby gentility but the bright and respectable colours of homespun—the báinín, the bréidín, the red flannel—will show their homely advantage. The use of white flannel and bréidín in smartly cut modern suits for the fine figures of the young men and women will give a new lease of life to native woollens. The nylon stocking appears to be irresistible and the knitting fingers are no longer busy at home for the protection of female ankles.

The celebration of festivals at holy wells and other places of veneration are not now occasions of jollification and are largely confined to devotional people of whom there are great numbers in Conamara. Pilgrims travel very often on foot to famous wells and shrines and will go on journeys taking several days. The custom of praying at holy places took deep root during the period when Ireland was being "perfected" and the Mass was forbidden and the pilgrimages preserve in popular memory the names of the early missionaries, of Pádraic, Colm, Bréanainn, Macdara, Feichín, Ciarán, Flannán, Caoillín and others.

The smaller gatherings of the visiting house, of the wake, of the wedding, and of the public house are infinitely the more conversational and entertaining, and when story-telling takes place, the pleasure of listening to the relation of magical deeds in fine words and phrases is so universal that the audiences are charmed into attention and silence.

Synge was greatly attracted by Gaelic talk. "I am in Aranmór," he writes, beginning his book, *The Aran Islands*, "sitting over a turf fire listening to a murmur of Gaelic that is rising from a little public-house under my room". He goes out of doors: "I met a few people; but here and there a band of tall girls passed me on their way to Kilronan and called out to me with humorous wonder, speaking English with a slight foreign intonation that differed a good deal from the brogue of Galway. The rain and cold seemed to have no influence on their vitality, and as they hurried past me with eager laughter, and great talking in Gaelic, they left the wet masses of rock more desolate than before."

Synge, who knew Irish and appreciated its edge and flexibility, left us no record of the conversations he heard on the road or through the crack in the floor. For a literary record of conversations in Irish we had to wait for the appearance of Máirtín Ó Cadhain whose dialogues and ruminations startle the reader with their closeness to reality. The recorded folk tales are in simple speech, delightful to hear, and pleasing to read, and full of examples for the story-writer and the dramatist, but it is in the common, everyday conversation and interchange that the subtlety and pungency of humorous and witty language appears. The habitual speaker of Irish may be entertaining or provoking at his will. The art of excellent, efficient speech is common, the give and take in verbal exchanges causes no anger and is a source of general enjoyment among listeners. If Synge had come down from his little room into the bar, or walked with the jolly girls on the road to Kilronan until his mind became saturated with the Irish word and phrase, as his soul did with the rain and the cold, he surely would have left us something more lasting if less fanciful than his plays, fine as they are.

I have not met many women who could tell any of the old tales, but women folk are gifted in conversation in their own little meetings at knitting or wool-carding, as you may judge from the frequent laughter of their exclusive gatherings.

THE CURRACH AND the samll and large sailing boats have served for fishing and transport, and the honourable trade of boat building has always been a necessity where men seek a share of the sea's harvest.

The simply constructed currach is the work of local men with a traditional craft. Its fragile frame and cover are put together with confident skill, and the handling of this long and buoyant coracle needs practice as well as courage It serves for fishing, for the towing of floating seaweed piles, and for transport from island to mainland and from shore to shore in the narrow bays.

The currach maker is not of course a master builder, but the builders of Conamara sailing boats have a claim to that title because of the durability and shapeliness of the vessels they construct. Ruskin might have found much to admire in the outline of a sailing boat of Conamara build. Her lines you must admire as she is moored or left high on the sands by the receding tide, and her balance and grip of the wave will give you confidence and a thrill as she moves to the force of the wind in her sail. The shaping, the joining, the staunching of her timbers have been done with great patience and skill, as the builder realised how responsible was his task, and delighted in achieving something near to perfection in his work. We can easily imagine how the tradesman was ever mindful of the wind and wave, how he reasoned why this and that should be so, how the tradition of centuries told him that it must be thus, and how he brought his work to perfection by following the examples and precepts of his predecessors. He selected and seasoned his timber with great care. The Conamara tradesmen used to travel far inland to pick, purchase and fell trees suitable for their purpose. The old boat builders all worked with deliberation, and spoke with a simple solemnity as if after reflection. It was a lesson in realism to talk with one of them, he contrasted so violently in his logical speech from the romantic language of the story-teller.

The maker of the great tales were not unmindful of the boat builders. In their descriptions the good vessel required strength and economy in her timbers, resilience in her spars and the speed of the March wind in her sails, a cable of silk, and an anchor unbreakable. The Fair Mariner was a master sailor on a vessel that never perished. He was able to sail into all seas, and once, he saw all the waters disappear over a mighty fall, and beyond which there was nothing but foam and spray, yet his good boat brought him safely home. She would fill the sky with showering spray but never a drop would damp her deck.

The sailing boat was often more expensive than the fisherman's house. The skill employed in its construction was at least as refined as that of the house builder, and skilled occupations are so few about our shores that the survival of this craft of boat building should be ensured.

The sailor who mans the púcán or gleóiteóg, and for whom the boat builder works, knows the narrow channels, the open bays, and the currents around the headlands and islands. Summer sailing off the western coast gives pleasure and adventure, and views that are unobtainable on land. It is not repeating a mere legend to say that real monsters of the deep seem on certain days to respond to our desire to catch a glimpse of them. The great whale we have seen off Ceann Gólaim, the basking shark in almost every inlet, and the porpoise in a great frolicking, leaping shoal in the North Sound.

Sailing in a turf or fishing boat, on a lively sunny day, down Cuan an Fhir Mhóir, or Cuan Cille Ciaráin, or from Clochnarón to the island of Macdara, or from any

49

shore at all to Aran or Bófinn, will repay in sea scents and sights and sounds, and in the experience of voyaging in the close company of a man who is captain and pilot of his vessel. The boatman in spite of his dangerous calling is calmer and also more exciting than the tailor or townsman who sits all day. The man on holidays knows so little about the sea that he finds a healthful humiliation in learning from a teacher who neither laughs at him nor patronises him.

Most lovers of the sea will sail for the pure pleasure of challenging the uncertain water, but in Conamara one must sail or miss visiting the islands made holy by the hermits who removed to them from mainland comfort and the temptations of security. The hermit saints of Macdara, Cruach na Caoile, and Ardoileán had practised the Franciscan precept of "want not," and their history may explain something of the people of Conamara, for these have never wanted very much, and their frugality and cheerful character may also have a lesson for present-day, hurried seekers of worldly comforts.

The visitor who wishes to see a local craftsman engaged in his trade may find it necessary to travel to Muighinis or Leitir Mór to find a boat builder, but there is one craftsman whom he will find everywhere. He will easily find a blacksmith busy in his forge with a mettlesome pony, or mounting cart wheels at the door. While the hardy little horse survives in Conamara the blacksmith will find work there. The poet Raftaire enumerated upwards of forty ordinary tools and articles which the smith he celebrated made in perfection, but the shops now supply almost everything. Modern centralised industry, while it multiplies agencies of distribution, has the effect of destroying the solitary tradesman. The tin-smith has had to go below the lowest standard of comfort and live in the open in order to survive, but the blacksmith who will farm or fish in his idle days has a greater security.

Iron is a metal of magic, according to our old traditions, and the blacksmith's calling was regarded as sacred, if not secret also. Men will repair a gate without regard for the carpenter, many men will patch a shoe without paying tribute to the cobbler, and every second man will build a wall without fear of the *saor*, but no man of sense will usurp the trade of the smith without paying the penalty, for the smith holds the secrets of his trade.

The blacksmith may owe the solidity of his character to his long association with the proud animal that first enabled world conquerors to set out on their never-ending wars, and to his services in the production of war weapons now obsolete. He was a fine maker of pikes while pikes were useful, but the romance is fading out of his trade, unless we regard as something romantic the forging of small anchors for the sailing boats, or of the holding irons for their masts. The skill, however, remains in the smith's hands and he remains the most useful craftsman in a rural community. It is strange that he seldom rides a horse, and that he is a poor storyteller, but one Conamara blacksmith of Cornamóna had a wealth of Irish songs which were faithfully recorded by the two gifted brothers, Tomás and Micheál Ó Máille. His name was Breathnach, and the Breathnaigh were so long associated with the working of iron that they became known as *Breathnaigh an Iarainn*.

Why the smith is but a poor storyteller is the subject of an ancient tale. When Cuchulainn discovered that the man he had slain in one of his single combats was Conlaoch, his son, a great sorrow overtook him and he resolved that never again should their swords be on opposite sides, and decided to have his own and that of Conlaoch welded into a single weapon. The smith to whom he came demanded a wage, and the wage was that Cuchulainn should tell a story in the forge while the finishing, the less clamorous part of the work, was being done. To this Cuchulainn agreed, but on condition that no woman should hear his tale, for he was in a rage against all women because Conlaoch's mother had forbidden him to disclose his identity to the father who had deserted her. The telling of the story began next day, but before Cuchulainn had arrived the smith's wife had concealed herself beneath the bellows that she might hear the recital of the hero. In the course of the tale, which was known to her, she interrupted Cuchulainn to correct him in some detail, and thereby betrayed her honourable husband and her own presence. It is said that the rage of the Hound of Ulster knew no bounds, and that a curse fell on the smith, and on all smiths, so that no man of them can ever tell a good story.

There are many weavers between Galway and Ceann Léime but I know of only one woman weaver, and she may be called the queen of the loom since she had no feminine rivals. She resides and exercises her undoubted skill in the parish of Rosmuc. In earlier times many women were engaged at the loom, and the cottage woollen industry still depends on their deftness of hand in carding and spinning. Men do the shearing, and pack the fleeces for sale, when they are sold. The teasing and carding is done entirely by women. Their technique has come down from the time of Abraham, and beyond, and their spinning on the large wheel produces the yarn for flannel and bréidín and for the socks of the boatmen and shepherds, and the workers who dig and mow. Garments made of homespun yarn are more lasting and comfortable for those who wear them than machined goods. The spinning-wheel thread will not run in the machines, and machined yarn never gives the tweed or flannel or footwear best suited to the open-air worker. One of the most admired accomplishments of women was that of the fine-fingered spinner, and the Irish Countrywomen's Association should find a fair missionary field in Conamara where weavers are ever calling for more yarn.

The colours we so much admire in many bréidíní are often due to the knowledge of natural dyes possessed by women who produce them from wild plants and blossoms. This knowledge is not very general but some of the older women are skilled in the production and use of natural dyes, and they are not wanting in the art of peppering yarn with a lively shot of blue or red or green that relieves the *glascaorach* and gives it a commercial value. They make no secret of their art, but, on the contrary, they will exhibit at the annual show the blossoms of the furze, the bramble and the heather, the root of the wild iris, and the stonecrop gathered off the granite, in proof of the honesty of their work. The red of the famous flannel is not from a natural dye.

When the yarn is finally prepared the careful spinner measures it, and reckons the number of threads needed for the width and length of the cloth she requires, and she divides it accordingly in exact lengths for the loom. The woven cloth needs thickening, cleaning and pressing, and most of this finishing falls to the woman worker who began the long process with the carding.

Once over a century ago poor weavers raised their charge a farthing per yard, but there was a price control they had not reckoned with. Members of the *Toraidh* association (the Terry Alts) took them out individually and thrashed them soundly. Mac Suibhne, the poet of the hills, made a song in their dispraise, and the weaver would have fallen into permanent ill-fame had not another and better poet, Raftaire, produced a poem in which he is described as king of the trades.

53

In those days of the poets every parish had a dozen or more looms. The only foreign cloth coming into the Conamara market was brought by the smugglers from Guernsey, but the local weaver was kept busy, for Guernsey cloth was expensive and unsuited for workmen's wear. After smuggling had been suppressed came the flood from the woollen mills and the cheap shoddy, but the local weaver long survived and has left many successors who still cast the shuttle and produce the homespuns worn by thousands all along the coast from Bearna to Carna and Ceann Léime.

This account of workers in wool has not done full justice to the busy hands of woman. Cardigans and costumes of neat make are produced by girls at knitting schools, and piece work is done in the home. The finished goods are marketed by Gaeltarra, a Government agency. The short wool of the little sheep is suited to carpet making. Large carpets have been produced in Conamara, and the small hearth rugs, made more generally, are admired and purchased by visitors.

THE LOBSTERMAN

OUR HOST IN Iorrus Aithneach took us for a walk to Muighinis on a January evening. It was January the 5th the eve of the Epiphany, the Twelfth Night of Christmas, and the anniversary of the Big Wind. The evening was mild; sea and coast in Muighinis were so luminous that we let darkness fall before we thought of returning, and lights were appearing in the scattered houses as we turned inland. Our way back led us past a house where we all were known. As the door stood open and was flooded with light from within we entered and were welcomed by man and wife and by a number of boys and girls in their teens. The whole Christmas season is one of rest, or of abstention from unnecessary work, and our visit was not regarded in any way as an intrusion. The woman of the house was a fine talker and full of understanding. Our inquiries of her husband concerning his fishing activities soon led her to tell how his industry had increased her

own toil. The harder he worked the more had she to spin and knit and sew. He was, of course, a great lobster fisher, but the business took all his time, and wore out all his clothes, and as the sea soaked him every time he went out she had always to have dry clothes ready. He spent days far from home cutting rods for the pots and came home from the shrubberies torn to rags. He spent weeks weaving the lobster pots, and when the lobster season began he rose before sunrise, and was out about the islands lifting the traps, extracting the fish and conveying them to the king-pot. The wear and tear of clothes caused by boats and ropes and the stones of the shore was beyond endurance. If her man would only remain at home and till his little fields as some others did she would have a rest from spinning and sewing.

One of us at least had a suspicion that her complaint was but her way of praising her husband's industry; and he also appeared to take it in that sense for when he got an opportunity of defending himself he protested that all the spinning and knitting was not for him, and he pointed to the smart cardigans worn by the girls and to the pullovers in fancy colours worn by the boys. His wife, he said, had but one fault, she was too industrious and could never be idle for a moment. If she was not spinning or knitting, she was carding or dyeing or doing piece work for the Department. She would never sit quietly by the fire and listen while a man told a good story. She might listen to a song if the singer had the right words and air, or she might sing to herself if she thought no one was listening.

The sarcasm was mild and did not annoy the good lady. She replied that storytelling was a poor way of entertaining visitors at Christmas time, and asked him whether he had consumed the quart of good whiskey she had purchased in honour of the *flaithiúil* season of the year. He protested his ignorance of its existence, and then she told him where she had stored it for safety and that he might procure it while she busied herself with the glasses. We left wishing success to herself and to the fisherman who prevents foreign raiders from stealing all our lobsters.

As we came out into the night it seemed as if the stars had fallen to the level of the horizon. A semi-circle of Christmas-candle lights shone in cottage windows on the heights from Coillín to Calafínis, and to Fínis itself, in the sea. Coillín, Leitirdeiscirt, Roisín a' Tomha, Carna, Síduach, and Ruisínnamainiach, remembering the Magi,

56

were all paying tribute and bidding farewell to the blessed season.

DISHES

NO CONAMARA MAN talks of food unless he feels the sharp need of a meal, but he enjoys rare, good dishes as well as any lord or ration victim who flies from the blessings of Empire to the happier plenty of the Republic. Mutton from the hills between June and Christmas is as pleasing as lamb in any season. Lobster is fresher at home than it can possibly be in London or Paris, to which cities we send quantities. *Muiríní* served in their shell for reality, with a crust of fried bread crumb and condiments, are better than turbot and wine on a lenten Friday. *Breallacha, sceanna* and *scadáin ghainimh* are delicious. A cook I once knew in Clochán used disguising sauces for shellfish without destroying the sea *blas* they should always have. The virtue of fish as a pleasing food lies in its freshness. Game requires days and days to make it tender, but fish is best eaten fresh out of the water. This is true of seafish as well as to the trout of fresh water. Salmon is a strong dish, but trout, white or brown, is delicate and always tempting even in this land of lakes. Carraigín had been commercialised and is no longer claimed as a special Conamara treat, but who will persuade the girls or the cooks to prepare a *toit bháirneach* or a *bruithneóg fatai* with the flavour which makes the old men lick their lips in memory when they talk of them.

I have longed often for a cake of fresh barley flour, but have never got it in Conamara. Barley was plentiful when poitín flowed freely, and the best storytellers who begin with the reminder, "*Is túisce deoch ná scéal*"—the drink precedes the tale—say also that a fresh barley cake, under its due share of fresh butter, is best when taken

57

with a generous cup of fresh milk with its due share of poitín.

I have eaten scones in Scotland, but, even if I were a poet, I would not sing about them. They left no memory with me to compare with that of the scones of Tír na Cille. These were served in free hospitality, hot from the griddle, with butter and the best of tea, after a long night's story-telling. Micheál Breathnach had come to see his old mowing comrade, Ó Mulrua, to tell him again of the Horse of Troy and the adventures of Mac Rí na Binne Brice. There were visitors from Dublin and Galway and in their praises they divided the honours evenly between the storyteller and the maker of the scones.

BEHIND THE BEANNA

A WALK IN the hill country affords an inside view that is sure to be more familiar than a passing look from the highway. The roadside scene tends always to be the victim of change, but the hills and the little valleys hold their own and do not disimprove. Going into the rugged hill country is like paying a visit to a house in a foreign land where you have not been before. If your visit be not too brief and your host be communicative you will take away a lasting impression of the dwelling and its inmates. When you travel behind the hills your visit may not be hurried for the simple reason that your progress is timed to a walking pace and you have time to listen and to see and observe. They way to Gleann Carbaid is a rough pathway that follows the river coming down from the upper Beanna into the lake of Coill Mhór. The pathway and river touch close to the Gleann Einín road, below Gleann na hEilte on the way from Coill Mhór to Sraith Salach. A lonely dwelling marks the beginning of the upward path. It is a rough uneven path but firm and free from mud and puddles, for the river frequently overflows and strong spates have washed away the turf and the earth beneath. It winds and turns with the rocky stream and never goes far from its singing companion. It gently ascends and is never steep, and has here and there a level stretch beside a pool in the stream. The pools in autumn make resting places for the white and brown trout on their way to the spawning beds. The trout are not easily seen when at rest, although the water is clear as crystal. A raven is circling overhead between you and the almost upright heights of the Beanna. Further along the pathway you will notice a dead or dying sheep for whose carrion the raven is waiting. No dwelling is in sight ahead until you reach the backbone of a ridge that shuts off Gleann Carbaid from the world. There, in the loneliest part of Conamara, are four or five houses, the homes of families who find a living in the most inaccessible of places where there is no level ground and no roadway for bicycle or cart. The stream tumbles along on its way from its source near the hill called the Cailleach. Close to the houses there is a double waterfall. A bowl in the rock halfway in the drop first receives the stream which churns and boils and again escapes. As we approached the fall an old man was sitting on the bank beside it. He was gazing steadily at the overflowing rock bowl and the noise of the falling water may have prevented him hearing our footsteps over the stones. When we stood beside him he looked up and said at once without surprise at seeing us, "I am counting the trout."

He pointed the stick he held towards the little waterfall, and instantly we understood, for there was a demonstration that explained how he was able to count the trout in the stream while we who had followed its course for over two miles had not seen one. A brown trout jumped out of the rock bowl to the upper stream, and immediately afterwards another fish jumped from the stream below into the bowl. "There's one a minute", said this watcher by the bank. We joined the watch and found that his reckoning was roughly right. The brown trout were passing up the fall at the rate of about sixty to the hour. The fish were small, none over a half-pound, but we saw no sprats. The current below the fall was too rapid for spawning beds to form and Nature was sending the mature trout up to the more level course of the river in the neighbourhood of the hog-back hill, the Cailleach, which we could see beyond Beann Fraoich and the other great hills that rise steeply here in line. The old man told us that farther up where the volume of the stream was smaller there was a long *fiodán* through which the water travelled underground. He said that the trout passed into the *fiodán*, but could not say if they went beyond it. My companion then told us that he knew of another such *fiodáin* on a little river. He had once made an opening down into it by digging a hole on the line of the water, which was near the surface. When he had removed the sods he saw the bed of the stream closely packed with trout lying side by side, and he filled a bucket.

The watcher was interested, but he did not tell us whether he had ever employed such a method of whether his *fiodán* in the hills had ever been raided in so primitive a fashion.

Beann Fraoich, a great stack of rock, is a compelling sight. Its upright posture distinguishes it from any other of the Beanna. The great shoulder slopes and wide bases of the other hills take away from their singularity, but Beann Fraoich on the Gleann Carbaid side has such a bold face that no ordinary climber dares attempt its ascent. As we stood contemplating its projecting brow a large bird, a grouse, flew out from its side, high in the air for a game bird. It flew rapidly and we soon saw a pursuer, a peregrine. We knew what the end would be and we saw the hawk descend and strike. The grouse fell like a stone, and the hawk soon found its prey in the heather.

As we returned we passed by a high bank the face of which showed a layer of peat above the stony gravel. Between gravel and peat there lay a long, sizeable tree trunk that had lain there for ages, and we remembered that a seanchaí in Mám had told us that Conamara once was wooded from Leitirfraig to Galway.

The high bulk of Beann Bhán stood over us on the right. From the road to Sraith Salach we could see the path of the climbers, but did not follow it, for Gleann Carbaid had blessed us with thirst and hunger and we hurried on. I recalled the journey, mostly on foot, made on his fast by Padraic Mac An Iomaire, from Cill Gaobhair beyond Cruach Phádraic to this very hungry spot. He crossed the Caoláire in time to hear Mass in the smallest of churches on the Líonán-Coill Mhór road, after which he faced the long tramp to Iorrus Aithneach. Another great walker came this way and ascended Beann Bhán. He was Seaton Gordon, the wanderer of the Highlands and Hebrides. He is an Albanach and had, I hope, more foresight in his tramps than had we, who took with us no *lón*. He has published an account of his climb and of the view from the summit—*Mullach an tsléibhe bháin*.

BIRDLAND

THE ATLANTIC COAST marks the most westerly line of migration for European birds. Proximity to the Atlantic and physical characteristics have made Conamara a rare birdland for visitors and even for ornithologists. The climate, which is modified by the Gulf Stream, is softer

61

and safer in winter than areas subject to the parching severity of east winds, and every inland frost increases the invasion of our feathered friends.

The gatherings of wild geese before departure in spring last for days. They leave in good travelling condition and the flights coming from the south-east towards the coast north of Ceann Léime are plainly visible in daylight, but are too high for the sportsman. Golden plover, more numerous than geese, dally in their leaving. Thousands assemble in a great hosting by Loch Coirib at the mouth of the Clár river and darken the sky with their practice flights there. The aerial performance is repeated at Aillbhreac near Ceann Léime where they halt on the last green hill towards the ocean. The native goldens separate from the migrants and remain behind to breed on the moors. The angler for early salmon on his tramp to the moorland lake will often startle brooding pairs out of the heather, if he does not actually see their eggs. The golden plover is not classed as a songster, but the trilling of flying flocks is one of the pleasantest sounds of the spring. We never witness the departure of migrant ducks but wild seas in winter drive widgeon and pochards in large numbers into sheltered bays where they may be seen close to the sheltering shore when winds are high. The writer saw over one hundred and fifty duck together in a small bay at Clochnarón where they were resting in severe weather. Mergansers are plentiful and widespread on lakes and rivers. They breed here but are not prized, nor is the large and elusive shelduck. The numbers of the mallard may be guessed at when in the breeding season a flock of over a hundred drake makes a line across the sky. The teal is less plentiful, but flocks handsome to see circle high at times over a favourite sheet of water.

Regular flights of cormorants from shore to lake and

contrariwise may be witnessed almost every day. A colony of tree-nesting cormorants for long held possession of an island in Loch Fada, near Clochán. The lake has a good stock of trout, but while the young were being fed in the nest the parent birds did not fish in the lake, but could be seen coming from the sea and feeding the young birds with saltwater fish.

Conamara has many heronries, some on tall trees, but many herons of necessity build in low bushes on lake islands. Fishermen tell of the great flocks of guillemot, razor bill and puffin that come to the near seas in spring. The maybird is vocal every night for a month when on its way to the northern nesting ground, and it is visible every day. The many tern colonies on islets and strands often include roseates and the little tern. Ringed plover, dunlins, oyster-catchers, godwits, turnstones, knots, sanderlings, redshanks and curlews, assemble on every strand, and watchers have frequently picked out the spotted redshank, the greenshank, and the grey plover, and the black-tailed godwit.

The gannet fishes in deep waters and confines itself generally to the greater bay. It may be seen ascending and circling before the dive, by boatmen and even by spectators on the shore. The great northern diver comes very close to land in most bays. The great-crested grebe breeds on Loch Coirib, and no lake with reeds is too small for the dabchick.

Conamara is a great home for gulls, the black-headed gull, the common gull, the herring gull, the lesser and great blackbacks.

The snipe breeds everywhere, woodcock in a few places, and the coast of Iorrus Mór receives the annual invasion of cock in late October. Grouse are so plentiful on some moors that there are lettings of grouse shoots, but partridge have always been scarce.

The solitary wheatear and the stonechat frequent every part, and the sedge warbler and willow warbler are not uncommon. Tits are seen wherever there are trees of any kind. The nest of the long-tailed tit was found at Mám. The goldcrest frequents Bailenahinse and probably other wooded places. Wrens, robins, thrushes, blackbirds and linnets find sustenance about the tilled patches and briar clumps on the fences. Flocks of redpole are very conspicuous in their flights when wild plants and weeds are in seed. The nightjar spins its *tuirne* in many lanes and no place seems to be too stony for the cuckoo, and no grass too coarse for the corncrake. The voracious starling does not despise the bits of moory meadow, but it meets a difficulty in finding suitable roosts. The flocks may be seen at late evening heading towards the bay on their flight to Aran, and there in winter they huddle about the warm chimney tops of the low houses.

The common crow is scarce because of the absence of trees, but the grey crow, jackdaw and magpie are common. The raven is nowhere numerous, but it is found in all the hill groups. The merlin, the kestrel, the sparrow hawk and the peregrine are often seen, the peregrine being especially fond of the high hills. The white wagtail on migration has been seen near Carna, and the snow bunting at Crosamháma. The rock pipit and the meadow pipit are very common, and the common sandpiper is found on almost every lake. Every rapid, constant stream in Conamara has a pair of dippers.

OBSERVERS

THE HASTENING, BUZZING motorist may see all of Conamara in a day. At any rate, he may see its limits and its
heights. A hustling American who had made his head-
quarters at Tralee set out to inspect in a day what there
was to be seen west of the Corrib. He was, on his return
to Chicago, able to lecture on his hasty trip. It is always
an advantage to walk, or even ramble through inhabited
places and make acquaintances. It is sometimes an inspiration to sit on a stone by the wayside when you find a
friendly man enjoying a smoke or a rest. When you
advance in acquaintance you may be offered a chair in
the kitchen, and once the conversation has started it may
end in a song or a story. The more you know of the Irish
language the better will be your enjoyment. You will find
the people very friendly wherever you go, whether to
Coisfharaige, or Ceathru-rua or Leitir Mór, to Carna,
or Clochnarón, or to the hill villages above Cornamóna.
The Chicago visitor might as well have passed over in a
plane through the stratosphere for all he learned in his
rapid passage. His countryman, Curtin, who recorded so
many old tales in Cill Ciaráin, knew better; so did
Larminie, who recorded stories as they were told, in
sound and sense. Stephen Gwynn of our own time paid
grateful and understanding tribute to the people whose
qualities he appreciated as few other writers in English
have done. Miss Edgeworth wanted a carriage and pair
even in the bogs, and poor dyspeptic Thackeray took
offence at his driver's singing in Irish until he realised
that there was a tune in the song.

The writers of the Lover school who created the stage
Irishman saw a dispossessed people as they appeared to

the eye, but grossly misunderstood them, or cared only to caricature them. The Dublin or English author could not understand why or how a poor man in plain clothes or in tatters should ever dance or sing, or be happy at all. They concluded that the merry Gael was but a funny freak who frolicked to amuse or deceive others, or to hide his exclusion from the good things the strangers had grabbed and held, even in their luxury. They represented the Irishmen as a merry Andrew or as a tipsy Tadhg and their caricatures created a school of writers not yet extinct. They knew little of the heart of the Gael or of the virility of the mentality that could survive the direst fate and make him capable of singing a merry song.

To those who can read in Irish, modern Conamara writers—they all are of our own time—offer many pleasant, revealing books. Pádraic Ó Conaire, whose Bohemian ways made him as well known in Dublin as he was in his native county, will be found the easiest to follow and the most versatile in his stories. The late Stephen Mac Kenna, a gifted critic of many literatures, held his work in high estimation, as he held the work of Pádraic Ó Domhnalláin to be in the good tradition of classical writers of Irish. Colm Ó Gaora has given us an autobiography which delights by its unhampered self-revelation. Séamus Mac An Iomaire took his native seashore for his subject and showed how faithful observation may be recorded without the shackles of science. The books of the late Professor Tomás Ó Máille are a treasury for all students of modern Irish. Pádraic Mac Piarais had by adoption made himself worthy of being classed among Conamara authors, and indeed his work has influenced Irish writers everywhere. The humility of his approach and his understanding of the people of the seashore have made Rosmuc known far beyond its narrow boundaries. Máirtín Ó Cadhain, one of the youngest of our writers in Irish, is already the most startling master of words that modern Irish had produced. Professor Corkery, writing of Ó Cadhain's last book, has declared that a giant has appeared in our literature. His power of language makes him appear at times to have forgotten the ordinary reader, as if he were writing for his own gamboling pleasure; but there is much more than word-weaving in his short stories. They offer a realistic and searching revelation of human life and toil in a land whose every pulse and feature he knows. Tomás Bairéad, our most prolific writer of short stories, comes from the Muigh Cuilinn district, which gives him a homely background for his work. His treatment of all his themes makes his books pleasant to read, for, like Ó Conaire, he prefers simple language, and has a good idiom. His nature sketches have given pleasure to readers who place true observation above imaginative pictures of wild life. Pádraic Óg Ó Conaire, in his books and broadcasts, has shown that he is a master of phrase and idiom.

A Holiday in Connemara, Stephen Gwynn.

Annála Beaga ó Iorrus Aithneach, Seán Mac Giollarnáth.

An tIomaire Rua, Tomás Ó Máille.

Antiquarian Handbook No. VI, Royal Society Antiquaries of Ireland.

Conamara, Pádraic Ó Domhnalláin.

Filí an tSléibhe, Tomás Ó Máille.

Irish Sketch Book, W. M. Thackeray.

Iar-Chonnacht, Ruairi O'Flaherty.

Ireland's Welcome to the Stranger, A. Nicholson.

Irish Folk Tales, Jeremiah Curtin.

Journal of Galway Archaeological Society.

Loinnir Mac Leabhair, Seán Mac Giollarnáth.

Loch Corrib, William Wilde.

Mise, Colm Ó Gaora.

Ordnance Survey Letters, John O'Donovan.

Peadar Chois Fhairrge, Seán Mac Giollarnáth.

Proceedings of Royal Irish Academy.

Siamsa an Gheimhridh, Dónall Ó Fotharta.

The Aran Islands, John M. Synge.

Tour in Connemara, Maria Edgeworth.

A SHORT GLOSSARY OF PLACE NAMES

Abhainn Bhalluisce .	. Owenboliska
Abhainn Chasla .	. Cashla River
Abhainn Chromghlinne	. Crumlin River
Abhainn Ghabhla .	. Owengowla
Abhainn Ghlinne .	. Owenglin
Abhainn Roibhe .	. Owenriff
Beanna Beóla . .	. The Twelve Pins
Binn Shléive . .	. Mount Gable
Caiseal . . .	. Cashel
Caoláire . . .	. Killary
Casla . . .	. Costello
Ceann Gólaim .	. Golam Head
Ceann Léime .	. Slyne Head
Ceathrú Rua .	. Carraroe
Cill Ciaráin .	. Kilkieran
Clochán, An .	. Clifden
Cloch na Rón .	. Roundstone
Cnoc Meá .	. Knockmaa (Castlehacket)
Coisfharaige . .	. The coast from Barna W. to Tully
Crosamháma .	. Maam Cross
Cruach Mhic Dara .	. St. Macdara's island
Cruach na Caoile	. Croaghnakeela
Cuan an Fhir Mhóir .	. Greatman's Bay
Cuan Chasla .	. Casla Bay
Cuan Chille Ciaráin .	. Kilkieran Bay
Cuan na Beirtrí Buí .	. Bertraghboy Bay
Cunga Fheichín .	. Cong

Dubhros	Dooras
Dúthaí Sheóigheach . .	The Joyce Country
Eanach Dúin . . .	Annaghdown
Formaol	Fermoyle
Gaillimh	Galway
Iomaidh	Omey Island
Iorrus Aithneach . .	Errisannagh
Iorrus Fhlannáin . .	Errislannon
Iorrus Mór . . .	Errismór
Leic Aimhréi . . .	Lackavrea
Loch Einín . . .	Loch Inagh
Loch Lurgan . . .	Galway Bay
Loch na Fuaighe . .	Loch Nafooey
Rinn Mhaol . . .	Renvyle
Ros a' Mhíl . . .	Rossaveel
Sraith Salach . . .	Recess
Uachtar Árd . . .	Oughterard